TI

URBAN

RITUALIST

To My Sister Rahema

Love you much, stay firm and stay well. I am grateful for the time we had, and look forward to better times in the future.)

Much Respect

Queen Afi Reynolds

2011

THE
URBAN
RITUALIST

A GUIDE TO
PRACTICING RITUAL IN
AN URBAN SETTING

Queen Afi A.N. Reynolds, M.Ed.

Outskirts Press, Inc.
Denver, Colorado

The Urban Ritualist
A Guide to Practicing Ritual in an Urban Setting
All Rights Reserved.
Copyright © 2011 Queen Afi A.N. Reynolds, M.Ed.
v4.0

All proceeds benefit the Universal Temple of Peace and Love Community Fundraising Project, www.utopal.org

Outskirts Press, Inc.
http://www.outskirtspress.com

ISBN: 978-1-4327-7049-5

Outskirts Press and the "OP" logo are trademarks belonging to Outskirts Press, Inc.

PRINTED IN THE UNITED STATES OF AMERICA

This book is dedicated to the Divine Energy of

The Goddess Sekhmet

O Sekhmet, Daughter of Ra

One who was before the Gods

Divine Mother of Heka

And Mother of Nefertem

O thou who art Sekhmet, Life-giver to the Gods

Sekhmet, Lady of Flame; Sekhmet, Great One of Magic

Sekhmet, Eternal is thy name! O hear me now!

Sekhmet, with Lioness Head; Sekhmet, whose color is Red

Sekhmet, Daughter of Ra; Sekhmet, Consort of Ptah

Sekhmet, Mighty is thy name! O hear me now!

Sekhmet, Goddess of Pestilence; Sekhmet, Goddess of Wars

Sekhmet, Queen of the Wastelands,

Sekhmet, Terrible is thy name! O come to me!

Sekhmet, Destroyer of Rebellions; Sekhmet, Scorching Eye of Ra

Sekhmet, Protector and Ruler

Sekhmet, Holy is thy name! O reveal thyself to me!

Sekhmet, Mother of the Gods

Sekhmet, Mistress of the Crowns; Sekhmet, thou art called Only One

Sekhmet, Beloved is thy name! Possess me now

O Great One!

Goddess of Healers, Physicians, and Priests. Known throughout the Universe

Ashe, Ashe, Ashe O!

ACKNOWLEDGMENTS

I first give thanks to the Divine Spirits who guided my hand in this work and gave me the vision and will to see it through. I give thanks, and all respect due, to my ancestors for their strength and guidance; my father Clarence Clarke Reynolds, grandparents Lardell and Ivory Shelby, my great-grandparents Ollie and Mack Shelby, Elizabeth and Mr. Gibson, and great-great-grandparents Rachel and George; my aunts Faye Shelby, Ella Mae Porter, and Mabel Harris; my cousins Terrell Porter, Vicky Cummings Smith, and Errol Keith Dorsey; and to all of the Coopers, Gibsons, Reynolds, and Clarkes known and unknown, those who have gone before and those yet to come; All Respect Due. I honor and give thanks to the communal ancestors who guided and encouraged me on this path; Baba Ishangi, Dr. John Henrik Clarke, Nana Kwame Atta, and King Sundiatta Keita, and the many others who set the foundation of reawakening African pride and greatness in the hearts and minds of millions around the world.

I would like to thank my family: my mother Rosemary Butler; and children Logombo, Anoa, and Amandla Potter; and my brothers Rodney and Clarence Reynolds, for their patience and support throughout the years. All respect due to my partner and teacher Grand Master Faouly Sekou Bomani for his love and acceptance of me as I stand at the threshold of my own awakening.

To my many teachers around the world, I say, Asante Sana, Master Kwesi Karamoko, Queen Mother Chief High Priestess OsunDara Nefertiti El, Dr. Shavi Ali, Dr. Theophile Obenga, Cardinal Mbyiu Chui, and Dr. Malidoma Some, and to the many others whose path I have crossed, again, Asante Sana.

AUTHOR'S NOTE

All products and services discussed in this book are available through the Universal Temple of Peace and Love at www.utopal.org, including Queen Afi's Natural Body Care Products and Ritual Works! Ritual Tools and Spiritual Counseling, and Grand Master Sekou's (Reverend Dr. Bruce Landers) Energetic Healing and Spiritual Leadership Training.

Queen Afi is available for interviews, workshops, group and personal rituals, and spiritual readings. Please contact her at spiritualdaughter@msn.com or at (313) 445-9832 for appointments. All tax-deductible donations to the Temple are greatly appreciated.

TABLE OF CONTENTS

INTRODUCTION

This book is the first in a series written to inspire those with a spiritual consciousness to cultivate their gift for the betterment of humankind through the practice of ritual. Rituals are Divine acts of faith that have the ability to transform and manifest. The practice of ritual is an art that heavily depends on the ability of the practitioner to feel and discern subtle energy within themselves and in nature, and to imagine and visualize.

To accomplish these ends, this book will focus on preparing the practitioner, physically, mentally, and spiritually to work in the energetic, ethereal realms within themselves and the universe. We will look at the tools that are available and methods that can be incorporated in an urban setting to energize the ritual practices that are already a part of everyday life (such as birthdays, marriages, baptisms, initiations, and funerals). *The Urban Ritualist* is by no means the definitive resource for the practice of ritual. However, for those who wish to infuse energy and higher purpose into the practice of ritual in their everyday lives or who are seeking a spiritual path, our hope is that it will help to restore a sense of normalcy among the gifted living in urban areas around the world. We hope to encourage their confidence to stand and be counted among those who seek to restore value to the pursuit of spiritual self-development, community and communal living, and respect for humankind's relationship with nature.

There are many great resources that I quote here and through whom I hope to inspire your further research and investigation on the subject. Most notably, I recommend reading *Let the Circle Be Unbroken* and *Yurugu*, by Dr. Marimba Ani. This is an excellent, brilliant exposé on the necessity of maintaining our spirituality in the midst of an economically and politically dominate culture that devalues it and the African worldview. For a more solid foundation and over-standing of the basic differences between the African and European worldview and perceptions, this book, along with Drs. Yosef A. A. ben-Jochannan and John Henrik Clarke, will add to a solid understanding of the role spirituality holds in the African ethos. Another path of study will be in Black African spirituality, which will take a little more digging, but that is critical in developing a sound basis from which to begin your practice.

Whether your spiritual consciousness is imbued from before birth, is the result of an initiation process, or is another step in your personal transformation, it is hoped that this book will help ignite the spark of understanding the importance of practicing ritual to enhance the development of one's relationship with Spirit and their Divine energetic selves. The most important point of the book is to inspire everyone to know and value their Spirit, and understand how a conscious relationship with Spirit can energize and transform their lives.

As the universal energy shifts and changes, many people are experiencing profound manifestations of Divine Spirit. In the past, it was easier to forget or hide these experiences in an effort to appear "normal." However, for those people who we call the Star Children, it hasn't been so easy. Attempts to deny these experiences have led many living in urban areas to manifest physical dis-eases and mental imbalances. Some have heeded the inner call and have begun to re-search for their spirituality either in books or on the internet. Others are able to travel to other countries to sit at the feet of enlightened ones and study their paths (a friend recently introduced me to the phrase "trust-afarians," trust fund babies with the resources to travel the world seeking enlightenment until their families pull the purse strings).

One can read a thousand books about spirituality and ritual or take a hundred classes and workshops, but until you commit yourself to a spiritual path, practice it, and are transformed by it, it is "dead" knowledge and simply takes the place of intellectualized religion. Ritual is to be lived; it must encompass your every thought and action every day of your life. Everything you do, touch, or feel should be imbued with spiritual energy; to see and feel Spirit in a thing or experience, and to think about Spirit and its depth of influence on everything is truly being Divine.

One of the first lessons is unconditional faith in the power of Spirit and the assurance that when the student is ready, the teacher will appear, even in an urban setting. They just appear in unexpected shapes and forms, and sometimes at the most precarious times. One is also led to understand that the most important teacher is your Divine Spirit. The importance of developing your Divine Spirit to operate at its optimal, and cultivating a relationship with your Divine Spirit is preeminent and is the first step in the practice of ritual.

In Western cultures, Spirit is considered abstract and thereby less valid than mechanical operations or intellectual experiences that can be easily analyzed, classified, and categorized. The practice of magic is considered heathenish and demonic while the practice of war and hatred is considered justified. I will not utilize space here to debate these points; however, it is important to fully understand where you stand on such subjects and, as a conscious civilized human being (one who lives in peace) how you conduct your life to fit your worldview and values.

Many will say that you are not living in the real world and that this Spirit world thing is dangerous. It is that, and more. That is why it is important to be clear in your intent for engaging Spirit and to have your shields up and energized. And, at some point in your journey you may find that it is the most meaningful work you could ever undertake. You may experience a deep-rooted sense of joy and accomplishment when doing ritual work, and you will know that this is the only work you were meant to do.

Even though there maybe a specific energy that a Ritualist communicates with, the work encompasses all manifestations of the Divine Energy. Your cultural heritage will play an important role, but we encourage the reader to "go with what works for you." Every culture has a history associated with the community/familial rituals that are practiced. Putting your energy into researching and uncovering that history is an act of sacrifice that will energize your practice. You feel a oneness, an expansiveness that energizes you and brings you civility (peacefulness).

This book was written based on my own life and experiences with Spirit and ritual practice, but again, is by no means a definitive guide to the practice of ritual. The tools and uses are based on my own experiences, not as an authority, but as a practitioner.

Chapter 1

MY STORY

I have lived a life that is different, odd, and confusing; yet exciting and blessed. I learned you make your own destiny, and that your destiny is in the making every day. I was born in 1956 to a self-educated Pan-Africanist father and closet intuitive mother in southern France. My father lived an even more different life. He was born in Puryear, Tennessee, into a family known for their distilling prowess. His father died when he was young, and stripped of any inheritance, he was shipped off to Chicago on the bus. Angry and alone, my father fell into trouble with the law and was eventually adopted by a single mother with one daughter. He enlisted in the Army, where he was eventually transferred to the Criminal Investigation Unit in France at the age of 30.

What inspired my father to educate himself about African culture I can't say. I know that he was a Garveyite and lived by Garvey's tenants to give African people, enslaved in America, land and independence. He expressed his willingness to work with anyone who worked toward securing land for his people. He studied the Moors and the Masons, and ran a chapter of a Pan-African organization while stationed in Germany in 1964. He was always involved in a business, and he believed in the necessity of being a business owner and self-sufficient in America. While still in Germany, we had a Blues Nightclub and Soul Food Restaurant, specializing in fresh chitterlings and live entertainment, and another club that no doubt featured my father's favorite enterprise—gambling.

When we returned to the States in 1966, he immediately went to work as an "entrepreneur," always from the ground up. He always held true to his purpose—find a land where Africans from the Diaspora can live secure and free; and learn to love and be proud of themselves, their culture, and their heritage to regain their true nature. He instilled this love for culture and heritage in my brother and me with stories of great African societies and leaders. He told us that we were descendants of royalty, and that he expected great things from us. He trained us to appreciate the arts and cultures (he spoke several languages) but we were expected to act like royalty at all times. He did such a good job in raising us with a knowledge and appreciation of our culture that he had to sit my brother and me down days before we left Germany and explain to us why African people in America don't like to be called African, and had to give a lesson on the different terms that were used by Africans in America to define/describe themselves. We settled on the term Black as the most acceptable to our way of thinking. Needless to say, we were very confused and made several slips in the first couple of months back in the States. My friends came up with an explanation of why we seemed so different from the other kids in the neighborhood and would tell them, "It's not their fault; they're foreigners."

My father was determined to do something great, coming

from what he considered a life beneath him. Through his consistent study to "know himself," he came to have a deep-rooted love for himself (I believe from his mother's side) and a fearless love for all Africans. He had a vision, different from a dream, and he worked tirelessly at manifesting it; even to the point of planting that vision in the hearts of his children to carry on. He was of royal blood; he was stern and strict; and most of my life, I felt like a recruit … no, lower than a recruit; and he showed me discipline, honor, humility, arrogance, and compassion, along with a little "Art of War" thrown in for good measure. To serve your people was the highest purpose one could attain.

My mother was born in Call, Texas, to a very close-knit family. Her grandfather was a landowner and well respected in the community. His land was divided into three farms, one for each of his sons. My mother grew up on her father's land with her mother and four sisters. She spent time with her maternal great-grandmother Rachel, who was of Scottish or Irish descent. Grandma Rachel studied herbs and healing from an escaped Native American named George. They would routinely go off into the mountains for days gathering herbs to fill her medicine bag. My mother too was different in many ways. She discovered early that she had the gift of foresight and could read people's intent; but she also learned that such things were considered crazy, so she kept her gift to herself.

Her father was disturbed about the quality of husband material in the South and went north to give his girls a better life. A spiritually wise man, I saw my grandfather read the Bible three times a day, but his knowledge of spiritual teachings was deeper than the Bible. He studied spirituality. When I made the decision to stop going to church, he continued to teach me on a deeper level and taught me to read the mysteries and allow divine revelation to guide me. He encouraged me to read the Bible from cover to cover, and in so doing, I saw the levels of understanding that reflected the true power of the Word.

My grandmother held fast to her Southern roots and learned at an early age to be self-sufficient. She was an excellent cook and seamstress, and earned extra money making hats. She once told me never to give up on life because you never know what life has in store for you. And her life was an example of that. She had lost both parents and her older brother at a young age, and was raised by Grandma Rachel. She married my grandfather at the age of 15, raised five very confident daughters, and had a beautiful home "up North," where she regularly entertained family who visited from the South. In her lifetime, she travelled to Germany, Rome, Israel, and Egypt. Not bad for a poor girl from Jasper County, Texas. She taught me how to cook and sew, and why she always said "fair, and you?" when asked how she was doing. There are times when I catch myself twiddling my thumbs just like she did, and I know she's talking to me every time I enter a kitchen.

My mother was a professional secretary and took great pride in her work. She taught me the tools of the trade when I was 14 years old and said, "I will teach you what I know so that you will always be able to support yourself." My mother travelled all over the world, spoke several languages fluently, and had the guts to walk away from a bad marriage. Her gift afforded her an opportunity to manifest her desires, which for this Taurean, was security and family. She barely refrained from love or a good laugh. She was always supportive of my gift and encouraged me to keep a diary of my dreams, never letting on that she possessed the same gifts; she just always seemed to understand. My mother was a quiet activist. She would go along with the program until you "insulted her intelligence" or tried to act superior, and then she would let you have it, both barrels blazing. She taught me to respect authority, but to always speak my mind. She taught me to stick up for the little guy, to use my intelligence to make things better for everyone, not just myself; and that if I knew that I was right, to never back down from anyone. I was born to this unlikely pair for a reason. My mother reflected the wisdom, my father the genius of African people.

I have memories of being swaddled in a blanket and carried down to the river near our home in the south of France by my caretaker, Madame, for repose on the lake in a boat owned by her friend (I think he was sweet on her; he would even serenade us). I remembered that I had been really close to a powerfully nurturing energy along with other powerful Spirits. I remembered that I used to do something with my fingers and toes that caused them to vibrate with the most delightful tingle, and I spent hours trying to re-create that feeling to no avail.

When I was six, I understood that my dreams came true, and I could hear sounds and people talking to me at night. At eight years old, I had a dream that I was listening to an Armed Forces radio announcement that J.F.K. had been shot in Texas. I jumped up and ran to my parents' bedroom shouting, "They shot John F." My father came out, looked around, and asked how I knew this, to which I replied, I heard it on the radio. The radio sat in plain sight on the kitchen island, and realizing that it was turned off and that I hadn't turned it off, I looked at my father who had that familiar "it was only a dream" look. But in a surprising move of "I'm going to give you the benefit of the doubt," he turned on the radio, only to hear music playing. As if relieved, he explained that if the President of the United States had been shot, they would not be playing music. Just as he finished those words, the announcement came exactly as I had heard it in my dream. He turned to my mother and said, "That's your child, deal with her."

During that time, I had certain memories of things that I couldn't explain. One day while driving through the German countryside, my brother looked out the window and exclaimed how unique and beautiful the sunset was. I looked out the window and interjected that I had seen sunsets way more beautiful than that. My mother turned to me and asked, "When?" I couldn't respond, but I knew that what came to me at the moment I saw the sunset was true. I had seen more beautiful and unique sunsets, I really had, with other planets coming into view over the horizon. I give thanks that I remembered.

When I was 15, I had my first awake teaching from my divine self: The most important part of me was not the part that I could see in a mirror, but what was inside of me. At that instance, I knew that I had to find out how to nurture what was inside of me just like I nurtured the outside. At 16, I began to practice a Buddhist meditation chant that helped my divine self flourish and even rise up. By the time I was 19, I understood that my divine self was a true ally and guide. In my twenties, I began to play with Spirit, listening to other people and projecting thoughts out, occasionally using my ability to hear my divine self-guidance to benefit others. I give thanks that through my rebelliousness, Spirit never forsook me or I it.

In my middle and late twenties, I began to meditate regularly while walking through the hills and valleys on the island of St. Thomas in the Virgin Islands and felt my divine self was being strengthened and could manifest itself outward. On one particular day, I was in a walking meditation going up a mountain past a home that housed two extremely large and angry dogs. As I was passing the house, I could see from my peripheral vision one of the dogs bolt from behind the side gate onto the road. Without any emotional or mental reaction, I lifted my right arm over my head and as my arm came down in front of the dog, he skidded to a halt and retreated, yelping like he had been hit. I never touched the animal. It was also during this time that I fulfilled a request from my grandfather to read the Bible for myself. I was given the King James version by my ex-husband and was told if I had any questions I could ask him. I had already formulated how I would accomplish my goal, to read the Bible from cover to cover, and was immediately inspired to understand that my divine self would disclose all that I needed. I set out to follow an old Rastafari adage, "a chapter a day keeps the devil away," and read one chapter every day. If there was something I didn't understand, I meditated on my desire to understand, and either the day's experiences would reveal an insight, or when I reread the chapter that evening, the insight would manifest itself clearly.

It wasn't until I was in my early thirties that I began studying Tai Chi and felt my Divine Spirit was pleased. I began studying Kemetic Yoga in my mid-thirties, and it changed my life forever. Having refrained from sexual relationships for seven years, the postures, breathing exercises, use of hand movements, and words of power (hekau) elevated my divine self to another level of vibration. I began to feel kundalini fire (sexual healing energy that radiates from the sacral chakra) and saw that with additional practice, I could learn to funnel that energy throughout my body and finally into my crown chakra, which allowed my divine self to rise for the second time in a trance state. I was in total darkness, dark matter/melanin, and could see a vision from another place deep within. I began to interact with spiritual beings, understanding that it is necessary to ask questions as well as learn, and understanding what it meant to be tested by beings from other realms.

At 46, almost 30 years after my first practice began; I was divinely led into the realm of ritual, as pre-cognized by Baba Ishangi, a powerful priest/shaman, and began studies of various forms of ritual and divination. Shortly after that, I experienced physical possession of a cat energy and began to study my Divine Mother, the Goddess Sekhmet. After years of meditation on this energy, I asked for a teacher of the shaman's way and love, and at 52, I met my teacher, a martial arts Grand Master and shaman/energetic healer. It was then that I heard my second life-altering message: when you give to Spirit, you have the right to receive. Through our energetic healing work, I have interacted with several beings from this and other dimensions. I have learned not to be afraid, and that I am in control of what I see and do. For the first time in my life, I feel "at home."

Grand Master Sekou encouraged me to tell this story about spirituality as I have experienced it, and I give thanks for all. To give in to Spirit by doing the work is the greatest feeling I've ever had. It fulfills the feeling I was desperately searching for as a child. It is bliss, and I am honored to work with all the Spirits and energies of the universe. I have travelled to other dimensions and seen things outside of my imagination. It's great, it's divine; and when you re-member with the vibrations of the past and allow yourself to fold back into the universal consciousness, then, and only then, are you fulfilling one's true purpose. Now, the question is, in what state will you enter that consciousness? I have determined to enter at the highest state of health and conscious enlightenment. I give thanks that I still have 90 years to learn and grow my divine self.

Chapter 2

YOUR DIVINE SELF

This is probably the most important part of ritual practice and spirituality—your Divine self; the Spirit within and how you perceive its oneness with all things. How to care for it, cultivate and nurture it, and how to have a relationship with it are critical questions that are to be pursued by the aspiring practitioner. As one journeys to develop his or her Divine self, they must prepare themselves to step into a realm of universal laws, Divine energies, and alternate dimensions and spiritual realms.

Many beginning their spiritual journey have been frightened by Western values and opinions about Spirit. Of great concern is the infiltration of and/or possession by unwanted energies, and how to know if a Spirit is harmful or benevolent. My response is that you have to develop a relationship with your own Spirit, and then you will be able to discern different energies without fear, and have the courage to walk and work in a spiritual realm or alternate dimension from a place of spiritual power.

Wayne Chandler's book *Ancient Futures*, brilliantly, outlines the Seven Hermetic or Universal Laws; but the student of ritual practices must also conduct extensive studies of the Dogon and other ancient peoples and their cosmologies to understand these long-forgotten and summarily dismissed concepts. Fortunately, we have many examples around the world in Native/Aboriginal peoples, or what the West considers third world cultures. I would prefer to go further back in earth history to more ancient cultures, that of Kemet, Ethiopia, and the Dogon. Although there is little clearly written history about these Black African cultures, the manifestation of what these cultures held sacred and the energy that they carry is still available for our use. The tools and methods created during that time in those places are still practiced around the world.

In ancient Kemet, one of the most highly espoused dictums and the basis of all knowledge and knowing was to "Know Thyself." In that physical and material knowledge, and spiritual and ethereal knowing, one was encouraged to pursue a deeper understanding of life from the microcosmic to the macrocosmic level, within and without, above and below. In the Metu Neter, Vol. 3, by Ra Un Nefer Amen, the highest law of God in the Paut Neteru represented the principle of Amen and espoused the concept of Hetep (inner peace), and that the natural state of humankind is to be at peace. Dr. John H. Clarke, in his speech on violence and the Western worldview, defined "to be civilized" as to be at peace. I would dare to say that to be civilized is to be in the Divine natural state of being, through or due to one's capacity to know oneself.

Another Divine law espoused by Maat (a Neteru or Divine Being in the Kemetic cosmology) and communicated to humankind by Djehuti (also known as Thoth or Tehuti) relates to the existence of a collective spirit or universal consciousness that consists of all of the energy and instances of consciousness ever experienced in this dimension. When one's own Spirit and consciousness is cultivated and nurtured to vibrate at a faster, more subtle level (which can only be accomplished by releasing one's Divine self), you affect the vibration of the collective and universal consciousness in a way that will promote spiritual awareness in others and the continued development of higher consciousness of self.

As civilized conscious beings, it becomes our duty to life (to our ancestors, the earth, Divine Spirit/Energy, and each other) to be our best, not out of blind faith, but by taking conscious steps to elevate our intellectual and spiritual selves. We go to school and spend a lot of money to elevate our intellectual selves, but where do we go and what are we willing to give to elevate our spiritual selves? Again, I must reiterate, the greatest spiritual guide is your own Divine Spirit, and by calling on that Spirit and developing a relationship with it, all can and will be revealed to you in a way that you can know and accept the truth of what is being revealed with clarity and trust. You should progress in your relationship with Spirit, listening and acting in accordance with what Divine Spirit reveals to you. It is a long process, hearing, listening, doing (being obedient to Spirit) with confidence and assurance that such obedience will be a blessing to you.

Let's examine some concepts that are fundamental to developing a relationship with your Divine Spirit from an ancient traditional perspective as revealed to me in my work with Spirit. First is the understanding that one must have confidence in the higher vibration of Spirit compared to the lower vibration of the physical or intellectual. Second, that there is such a thing as Divine revelation and wisdom, without the validation of Western academia. Once you embrace the reality of Divine consciousness, the understanding that it exists for the uplifting and transformation of humankind unfolds, and you can begin to examine how you are impacted by this Divine consciousness and how to use it.

In our current life existence, Spirit exists in relation to the mind, body, and environment, and these elements are critical to cultivating the Divine spiritual self. It is arduous work and takes years, not to master it, but to become consistent and committed to it. This is how to truly manifest results from spiritual and ritual practice. It may take years more for one to witness the manifestation, but Spirit and ritual cannot be regulated by time or space. They are in Divine order always.

The Mind

We do have the capacity to control our minds, our thoughts, and thereby, control our actions and feelings. The first step is to control our lives and thereby, manifest the experiences that we desire. Meditation, breath, and hekau (words of power) are the tools that can be used to quiet mundane thoughts, promote stillness and silence, and to expand and energize our conscious Divine selves. Abdominal breathing, along with visualization, is important in guiding energy and oxygen through our bodies. The process of oxygenation of the body is critical to warding off many medical diseases. Oxygenation of the brain increases its functioning, including one's ability to expand their mental capacity and clarity as opposed to mental activity. Clinical research conducted and reported in the book *Why Darkness Matters,* shows that the breathing technique, "alternate nostril breathing," or pranayama breathing, is effective in stimulating neuromelanin cells in the brain. Neuromelanin cells also influence one's conscious awareness of self.

There are many breathing techniques, and it's good to have a simple beginning exercise that will help you achieve calmness and expand your breath capacity. Begin with breathing patterns that are short and easy (counts of four seconds/ heartbeats on the inhale and the same on the exhale). Build on the pattern in terms of length of breath and number of repetitions. Progress to more complex patterns and expand the repetitions, but always achieve complete relaxation when performing the technique before moving on. Never practice breathing techniques while driving or operating dangerous equipment, but do take every opportunity throughout the day to practice.

The breath is a tool that can be used effectively in beginning one's meditation practice. By focusing on the breath, how it feels moving through the nostrils and above the lip, its temperature, which nostril it flows through, even its taste, occupies the mind and reduces random thoughts. It is important to understand that the purpose of meditation is not to eliminate thoughts, but to help you not become distracted by them or to consciously engage or focus on them. Thoughts will come and go; let them, then refocus on the breath.

The same is true when incorporating hekau or words of power. I begin my hekau by saying it out loud once, then intoning the hekau. You may be distracted by random thoughts, but as soon as you realize it, return to repeating your hekau. A hekau can be a chant or prayer that is intoned repeatedly, or divine sounds that have no known meaning and that create a vibration in the brain or body even when intoned. The sound "aung" is one such Divine sound that is said to excite the third eye chakra. The Lord's Prayer is also an effective hekau. As you continue to use your hekau, you will discover

that the hekau sticks in the "back of your mind" and instead
of intoning the words or sounds consciously, you can just
hear them ringing in your higher self.

There are hundreds of breathing patterns and combinations
of words and sounds that can be used, but the most important
thing is to 1) remain totally relaxed, 2) start out with simple
breathing patterns, and 3) research to understand what part
of the body and mind the Divine sound will affect. In the ap-
pendices, I have outlined some breathing exercises and patterns and hekau that I have used.

The Body

The highest level of physical development must occur on a
cellular level to truly be transformative. It is important because a fit body will aid in the release of Spirit and allows
energy to move through the body uninhibited by pain and
disease. One's diet and exercise regimen greatly impacts the
fitness level of the body, so it is important to do the research
necessary to determine the healthiest diet regimen and most
efficient exercise program for you.

I would caution everyone at this point to always be gentle
with yourself. The adage "no pain no gain" is not appropriate for spiritual development; rather "slow and steady wins
the race" is more appropriate. I encourage everyone to be
gentle with themselves and not beat themselves up, physically or mentally. Know that you are a child of the Divine
universe, and that you are loved by your ancestors.

Diet and exercise are deeply related to one's values (intellectual) and belief (emotional) system, which is indicative of

their style of living. When you desire to change your diet and exercise regimen, you are attempting to change your values and beliefs, which requires you to examine and transform them on the spiritual level. The diet and exercise regimen that you choose is indicative of how much you value yourself and the world around you, and whether you believe you play a direct role in or have the ability to affect yourself and the world around you. An optimal diet and exercise regimen must foremost consider the whole person; this is determined by astrological indications, blood type, family history, and current body condition.

By practicing a variety of exercise modalities, one can develop a body fitness regimen that is most effective for them based on age, physical stamina, and environment. In Kemet, I believe that yoga was one such tool that was developed to enhance spiritual development. If we look at the sun salutation, one can see how 10 postures (aligning one's body to tap into cosmic/universal energy) are linked together, along with one's breath and focus, creating an energy flow from one posture into the next and back again to the beginning posture. I believe we are seeing the true holistic nature of what all yoga should be. The practice of yoga as flowing postures also helps facilitate trance and allows one to experience transformation in how they perceive themselves in society and how they interact with other life energy.

In today's yoga practice, devotion, service, meditation, breath work, hekau (or mantras), and hand gestures (mudras) are practiced separately. In Kemet, I believe that all of these components are a natural progression of the practice of the postures and they work together to heighten one's personal experience with their Spirit, and promote internal stillness that translates into an ability to perceive Divine revelations and stronger intuitive awareness. The final outcome is the consciousness of Divine self and one's true nature, and purpose. The physical effects are the ability to totally relax and to allow the kundalini energy to stir and rise through the entire body on a cellular level to activate the other chakras and promote healing.

Exercises that assist in the development of one's breathing capacity, joint flexibility, and mental focus are a great asset to achieve the physical stamina needed to conduct kundalini energy. Forms such as qi gong and tai chi are a progression of yoga forms, and are more specifically designed to aid in the successful development of the outer energetic bodies and the cultivation of one's ability to manifest change in their life energy and, by extension, their experiences.

One's diet is also critical to nurturing the spirit. It is important to feed the body food and water that has nutritional value and to maintain a balanced diet. It has been shown that blood type, one's astrological sign, body type, heredity, and environment are all factors in determining which foods are best digested by your body and which can provide the most nutritional value for your energy level. Studies are being conducted to determine the role melanin plays in diet on an individual and cultural basis.

A meatless diet may be more effective in obtaining optimal health; however, an understanding of the power of thought and intent in regards to what we put in our mouths should also be valued. Our Divine selves can be developed to the point where we can eat or drink the worst of food stuff (that lacking any nutritional value) by infusing the food with instructions to heal and the body and with instructions to assimilate and eliminate in an effort to attain our necessary nutritional goals. Because food comes from the earth (which is the best source of food), it carries the same energy as humans, and that energy can be manipulated on a cellular level both in the food and in the human body. In order to most successfully accomplish this, you must fully "Know Thyself." This is why it is important to energize your food with your intent while preparing, serving, and eating. The determination of effectiveness must also take into consideration the value one puts on preserving their life energy at all levels of physical manifestations.

Many people (myself included) cook with their ancestors. We use this time, meal planning and preparation, to communicate with that ancestor who was especially skilled in the culinary arts, calling on that energy and listening to and following their instructions. We will discuss ancestral feeding— a ritual to give thanks to that ancestor for their assistance, nature for its role in growing the food, and the preparer. As we partake of our food, tradition dictates that we pray over our food, but as conscious beings, we should be praying with every bite, imbuing our intent to receive complete digestion and healing energy from the food. This is all a part of preparing the body to more fully interact with Spirit/energy and beings from other dimensions.

The Environment

It is in the practice of these body and mind tools, the performance of rituals or recognition of Spirit, that one creates an environment that promotes internal and external peace and the ability to be in harmony with Spirit. It reminds me of the saying, it's easy to be at peace when everything around you is going your way, but can you maintain your peace when everything around you is in chaos? There are a few points to be made about the role your environment plays in cultivating your Spirit self:

- Recycle constantly, keeping things at a minimum. Cluttered surroundings indicate a cluttered mind and a cluttered life; one filled with outdated and irrelevant relationships, thoughts, and actions. When we hold on to old things, we stagnate our thoughts and speech and are unable to realize our transformed future selves.

- The Universe always seeks balance, so if you are blessed, pass that blessing around; if you realize some growth in your higher self, celebrate it by giving to others. If you try to hold on to your blessings, the act of regaining balance says that some unexpected experience will come into your realm to take something away, so give freely the more you are blessed by Spirit.

- Create an atmosphere and mind-set of thankfulness. Give thanks for all that you have, no matter the condition. Be thankful and praise it and the universe for blessing you with more. Care for all that you have, and show yourself ready and able to receive more in humbleness.

Spiritual Baths

An important aspect of living and working in the spiritual realm is to construct a mechanism by which you can energize and protect yourself. We use spiritual baths before doing spiritual work or for complex processes, we might bathe for 3 or 4 days prior and one day after. After an especially intense session, I will pour a solution of energized spiritual bath oil and water over my head, a sort of shock treatment. To clear any residual energy that might linger after an encounter or experience, I wash my hands up to the elbows and apply oils. It is important to be serious and committed to spiritual work, to know yourself, your strengths and weaknesses, and especially to be able to discern when your energy level needs work.

Personal Rituals

It's a good idea to have an arsenal of personal rituals that you can pull from for different experiences. Personal ritual consists of calling forth those energies that can assist you in preparing for your work and setting the stage for you to go into a trance. The ritual can take many forms, and as usual, it is the intent that you put into the ritual that gives it power. Choose a highly energized time, during a planetary alignment or cycle. Choose a combined meditation, breath work, and hekau regimen for several days before, and continue it throughout the spiritual work. Every layer that you add to the ritual re-enforces your intent and gives life to your quest.

A simple personal ritual is to write spiritual symbols or hekau on a piece of paper, along with your intent. Imbue the paper with your energy by blowing on it, dancing on it, sitting on it, then placing it under your pillow or bed to sleep on it. You can also fold it and place it in your shoe and walk on it for several days. Dispose of the paper by burning or burying it while repeating your intent.

It is especially important to follow Spirit during this process. You may have a personal ritual all worked out in your mind, but Spirit will guide you to create the most powerful and beneficial personal ritual for your spiritual upliftment. It is important not to get hung up on everything being perfect. Instead, use your energy to listen to Spirit's guidance while remaining flexible. The most important aspect of any ritual is your intent.

Retreats

Retreats are another excellent tool to reenergize yourself. Retreats should be relaxing and peaceful, and should allow you time to be with yourself and nature. To get the most out of the experience, you should limit your contact with the outside world and the number of electronics around you. You should also have and take the opportunity to perform rituals. Retreats also provide an opportunity to uncover spiritual or ritual tools. It's about giving of your energy to the space and having the right to take something from the space. This something should be energized with your intent and used in your ritual work. The idea behind having this connection with the retreat space is to be able to return to the imagery and energy of the space, anytime and anywhere, to give yourself a boost of peacefulness.

Chapter 3

SPIRIT AND CULTURE

The spirit of a society is expressed through the rituals that are upheld and transmitted through generations. The definition of culture is given in the context of biology and sociology. Common in both is the focus on growth and development; for biology, by using a nourishing substance, and for sociology, by using common ideas, customs, or "ways of living ... transmitted from one generation to another." I believe another factor or way of expressing culture is through common values, attitudes, and beliefs. How culture is expressed within a certain social structure varies. In ancient cultures, there are more similarities than differences in the values, attitudes, and beliefs held and transmitted in the people, which speaks volumes about what ancient peoples perceived as the critical ingredient in facilitating growth and development in all of the people in the culture—Spirit. Spirit/energy/vibration gives power to the manifestation of a culture. When Shamans all over the world speak to a plant or blow on it, they are confident that the energy that they put into that plant or is activated in it will manifest in the innate power of the plant to heal. When Asian women wear red at their weddings, as is customary in their culture, it gives power to the ritual of marriage and to the process of building a family and continuing a family line. The color red carries a lot of energy and is recognized in many ancient cultures as an energetic color that heightens the connection with power, action, the sacred, and the ancestral realm.

As a conscious Spirit/energy being, we are all descended from an ancient culture, and it is our responsibility to research, meditate on, and uncover our individual interpretation of how our culture is manifested by how we live and relate to other beings, with the planets, and the universe. Spirit and culture are inextricable foundations for a people united in a common bond and purpose. The purpose for ancient African and other "first" peoples is the elevation of the universal consciousness vibration/Spirit/energy. This vibration acts as the glue for human cells, the earth plane, and the physical universe. Studies are now being conducted, costing billions of dollars, to uncover the vibration needed to replicate dark matter (antimatter) which many now admit is the predominate energy in the universe.

If you look at the process of an expanding cell and the movement of magnetic energy through and around the earth, you will see a striking similarity in their operation and their function. The cell at the human zygote level consists of a cell within a cell, just like the earth is an iron sphere within the sphere of the planet. There are two energies/vibrations/ spirits (male and female) that circulate around the cell itself, and when the energies are directly opposite, they form a tube running north and south through the zygote cell. In a very similar way, the earth's magnetic energy/vibration/ spirit flows through the earth's poles, and according to some physicists, the flow of magnetic energy around the earth and through these poles is what keeps our atmosphere in place, which maintains life on this planet in the form that we now see. No other planet in our solar system has this same magnetic energy surrounding it, even though many believe that at some point they could have. So if the combined purpose of a people is to elevate this vibration/spirit/ energy level that is critical to sustaining life on this planet, their culture must contain remnants of knowledge critical to elevating the energy level and maintaining life.

Our ability to trace the cultural development and spiritual practices of many "first" peoples has been systematically jeopardized. Whichever ancient culture you trace your heritage or DNA to, pursue a deeper understanding of the basis of that culture. In the case of ancient Kemetic culture, the task is made even more impossible since it is a culture that is no longer consciously practiced and the language no longer spoken. The writings that have been exposed for public view are still indecipherable by those of other cultures who profess to "know the truth."

The practice of religious factions to demonize these cultures and label them as being "heathenistic, primitive, animalistic, and uncivilized" set the stage for chaos to spread from the shores of Europe, through Africa, to the shores of America and beyond for the past 3,000 years. Taking into account that it took Europeans 1,500 years to get out of Europe, and that millennium prior to this same time, ancient Kemetic culture was being spread around the world—to Asia and Mongolia, across to North, Central, and South America, and back—it is no wonder that today, these European descendants have never been able to correctly apply the knowledge or fully understand and value this ancient culture. Our saving grace today for those who wish to follow in the footsteps of the ancient Kemetic ancestors and to "Know Thyself" is that their knowledge, critical to maintaining life on this planet, was transmitted to so many other ancient cultures that we are now able, through Spirit, to piece together and formulate a path to understand and apply the ways of this most ancient and Divine culture.

Toward this outstanding opportunity, I would like to submit the following premises that I deem well documented (I have constructed a list of references that should be studied) and accepted (in my mind at least) when studied from an African worldview, that I hope eliminates some of the hesitation associated with regaining our divine status as conscious and civilized beings and seeing the world through an unencumbered heart. The purpose of this journey for me was always to know the truth, because I know that we can only have peace if we start from a foundation of truth and respect.

1. World civilizations were built from the foundations laid in Africa, the spiritual wisdom from Ethiopia and the genius from Kemet/Egypt, dating back at least 4,500 years, at most 40,000 years, and were magnanimously spread throughout the known world by its creators.

2. This ancient foundation was systematically erased from the annals of humankind, and the knowledge plagiarized by men of lesser understanding and spiritual development; therefore, the ability to manifest the power inherent in these ancient cultures was lost.

3. Since these ancient times, there have been several efforts to systematically erase African people from the face of the earth: from the Arab and European invasions and subsequent enslavements of the descendants of these ancient cultures, and massive

destruction of the land, to the spread of disease and disease-causing organisms today.

4. The more brutal attempts occurred during the enslavements, where the African was further stripped of the basic elements that make up a personality or ego, their culture, their ability to communicate, their spiritual practices, their family/community structure, and their name which linked them to their ancestors. These traumatic experiences cannot be equated with any other event in world history. The fact that this trauma is still being inflicted, in any form, centuries later, and that the impact of such trauma is still being felt, at many levels, is a testament to the force of the chaos that has engulfed the African race for over 1,000 years.

5. This stripping of personality and culture continues to affect the ability of Africans, especially in the Diaspora, to know their true nature and express that nature in the global mix of cultures and worldviews. This affect is called Post-Slavery Traumatic Stress Syndrome, and I contend that this is the leading obstacle facing the African race. Our survival past 2012 depends on the ability of African scholars, physicians, and spiritualists to join together to construct a multilevel treatment program that is free and readily available to everyone, easy to implement in a small group format, and that includes the holistic reeducation, spiritual cleansing, and social reconditioning of our people, and it can only be done by us.

In these five premises, we have set a foundation for healing a people today—to know the truth of their ancestors, an ancient peoples with a higher understanding of what it means to be divine, and their ancient cultural ways. This foundation includes Spirit and magic. This culture must not be rebirthed disjointedly or in a schizophrenic manner. There must not be any conflicts between science and religion, education and magic, one person's peace and the peace of the world. This culture is a manifestation of the highest aspirations of human beings—to be Divine beings. It was the essence of the people and their collective spirit. In our examinations of the cultures of ancient history, we can see the customs, values, and beliefs that had the greatest impact on the survival of a people and their transformation to a higher wisdom. These are the aspects of culture that should be nurtured today. In the face of modern and future technology, it is a tall order, because it means ignoring what is comfortable, popular, and accepted for what takes determination and commitment to peace, love, and wisdom.

Today's modern cultures purport to be the reflection of the people. It is imperative that you take some time and look around you. What are the prevailing "norms" of your culture? How are people relating to one another? What do the people value? How are the people educated? More important, are the people in the society in which you live at peace, and what are the values that have been passed on through generations that they continue to uphold? Today, we are experiencing the results of 3,000 years of chaos. The practice of "forced conversion" left people without a culture or with the practice of their culture being deemed illegal. In its place, human beings were left with countries and boundaries, and the most dreaded of them all, contracts. Today, human beings live in countries that are founded on laws and constitutions that are based on fear and consumption. The clothes we wear, the food we eat, the homes we live in, the cars we drive, the education we get, the striving that we experience as human beings are rooted in fear and consumption. And as we move into a global society, a shift toward cultural degradation is following, where even the most sacred of truths that have been uncovered are demonized, popularized without the true meaning also being communicated, or made into the brunt of a joke. As consciously aware beings, we must take responsibility for the cultural values, beliefs, and norms that we walk, talk, and for which we stand. If we don't stand for something, we will continue to fall for anything. Now is not the time for straddling the fence. Our intent must be clear, as is what we stand for. Do we see reality in the eternal and spiritual, or do we put our faith is bricks, mortar, and politics?

Chapter 4

THE ELEMENTS

As urban ritualists, it is important to use the resources available to access the energy inherent in our natural world, the elements Earth, Water, Fire, Nature, and Mineral. Once again, it is the intent put into what you have to work with that manifests the power of the elements described below. The elements are natural phenomenon that occur throughout the universe and are manifested in every living being. They are our common denominator, and each possesses a distinct vibration and, therefore, distinct energy. By focusing one's intent, the energy of an element can be drawn upon, using representations of it or by actually interacting with the element. With proper techniques, one can go into the trance state allowing them an opportunity to connect with the energy of an element and to manifest that energy when needed. Your intent is the power that allows you to interact with these and other energies, and energies in other dimensions.

Each element emanates an energy that is expressed through the African and Native American Medicine Wheel. Although there may not be consensus on the elements (in Asian cosmology air and metal are included) and order or number association of the element, continued work with each element will reveal the root of the element and its relationship with the whole. The most important aspect of the elements is the relationship they have to one's need to feel conjoined and supported, to have harmony in their world, to take appropriate action, to assimilate and accept change, and to express themselves. The African system that I use is from the Dagara people of Burkina Faso, West Africa. In this system, the earth element comes out of the center of the wheel and the numbers 0 and 5 are associated with it. The water is at the north, encompassing over one-four of the wheel, and the numbers 1 and 6 are associated with it. The fire element is in the south with the numbers 2 and 7, and is a little smaller than one-fourth of the wheel. Nature is to the east with the numbers 3 and 8, and mineral is in the west with the numbers 4 and 9; each encompassing about one-fourth of the wheel.

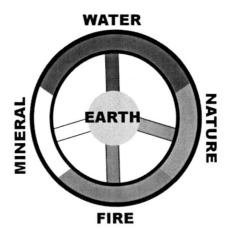

The Earth Element

The energy manifesting within the Earth element or Spirit relates to one's foundation or being grounded, and focuses on support from outside of self, especially the home environment.

Earth spirit speaks to the root of things and aids in conducting energy through our feet to energize our root chakra.

This process is also seen on a micro level where neuromelanin conducts energy through its tendrils, energizing and illuminating the neurons with information or vibration that is transmitted throughout the body. This is mirrored on a macro level where dark matter is pulling in and conducting energy through the universes, sending out information or vibration. The planet Earth is manifesting as a vibration of this dark matter emulation on a level that nurtures life as we collectively perceive it. On our earth, we can draw that energy up from the core or descend and be buried in it. You can access this energy by standing in dirt barefoot, but if you live in a concrete or fertilized lawn jungle, stand in a wash pan full of organic dirt. And if that doesn't work for you, get a plant and when you water it, stick your nose close to the dirt and inhale the aroma, then stick your fingers in the dirt and feel the texture. All the while meditate on the nurturing quality of earth and the flow of nutrients through the plant, knowing that the same happens for you from earth and the sun.

Use the Earth element as a means of grounding a request, especially of a physical or material nature, or energizing an item by burying the request or item in the earth. Earth can also be used as a medium to mix other substances with (ash, incense, and other fluids) and used in a talisman or medicine bag for protection and healing.

The Water Element

The Water element or spirit has two distinct energies manifesting within it: its ability to cleanse and its intuitive nature.

This duality is played out in the theme of reconciliation where blockages are removed and a new understanding arises to bridge conflicting views. This new understanding birthed from a deeper wisdom reveals solutions already inherent in those conflicting views. Water, being the most prevalent within and outside of us, has a very attractive nature and interacts with and is interacted upon by the slightest vibration. Tears as a form of expression transform us on a physical and spiritual level. The water that we take into our bodies can be transformed by mere thought. The importance of water, on a cellular and sub cellular level, has been well documented by scientific and religious studies.

If you don't have access to a body of water, keep a water fountain or fish tank around, or just sleep with a glass of water near your bed (infuse it with words of power and strong intent first) and drink the water in the morning with gratitude. Make your bath or shower time a sacred time by infusing your intent in the items that are used (candles, incense, oils, soaps), and listen for messages or insights while consciously washing your body.

For rituals, the most important use of water is in the pouring of libations, which should be practiced regularly. One method is to set a glass of water by the door with a plant and say a prayer over the water. In the morning before leaving the house, pour the water onto the plant acknowledging your ancestors and making your request. When you return home in the evening, you start the process again by setting a glass of water by the door and saying a prayer over it. Offerings can also be given to water, as the water's current is equated with the cosmic flow of energy and can carry a request to the spiritual realm. When you make a food offering to the water, you are putting into operation the cyclical energy of balance: feeding the fish, who defecate and feed other microorganisms and plant life on which the fish feed' mirroring your desire for your offering of goodwill and positive intent will be carried out into the universe for others to be fed and strengthened. Another ritual involves giving a person a spiritual bath, a task to be carefully undertaken. The intent of the person receiving the bath, and your intent for performing the ritual must be clear, and precautions taken to shield yourself before undertaking the process. Use a mixture of herbs and water that can be sprayed on the person after they have been cleansed to open the way to renewal or transformation.

The Fire Element

The energy manifesting within the Fire element or spirit relates to the active or masculine yang energy, one's ability to accomplish, build, generate movement and action, conquer, and dominate. It is power whether exemplified by our world of systems or by the ancestral realm and its systems. Fire spirit speaks to the ancestors, not in the sense of hellfire and brimstone, but in the sense of having the power to interact and make requests in the ancestral realm. Through fire, we speak to the ancestors and the ancestors speak to us. When one lights a candle, they are illuminating their thoughts and intentions in the spirit realm and putting fire or active energy into that thought and/or intent.

If government codes prevent you from building a bonfire, fire pit, or barbeque pit, using a single candle or several candles (with plenty of water around) will be a good alternative. The heat that emanates from incense coals and the smoke itself are also representative of the element.

In the ritual process, fire is a medium by which one can enter the trance state. By focusing on the flames of a bonfire or especially a single flame of a candle, and using words of power, it becomes easy to close off the intellect and allow the higher Spirit to emerge. Burning requests in fire as a way of energizing the request and releasing it into the spiritual realm also produces ash that can be used in rituals.

The Nature Element

The energy manifesting within the Nature element or spirit relates to one's true self and its ability to create and change your environment or reality. Spiritual energy is high in nature, making it fertile ground to energize your rituals. Nature is to be studied and its systems understood so that one can use the components of nature (trees, earth, water, air, sun, moon, stars/planets, insects, birds, and other animals) in rituals and as spiritual tools to energize our requests. Feeding animals, using water, earth, and trees as a medium, is one way to give blessings to balance our rituals and requests. Displaying an understanding of nature and its ecosystem will open you up to higher understanding of your Divine self. One should seek out nature and feel the energy inherent in nature … hug a tree, walk barefoot in the grass or sand, watch the animals and study how they live and work, look up at the sun, moon, and stars … become one in spirit with nature and thereby have true dominion over it.

In the ritual process, the ability to help the client see his or her true self. to recognize and accept change (especially the transition from life to death) and the cyclical relationship of past, present, and future, is the most powerful outcome that can be accomplished. Reflection on what is near and what is far away, including ideas and perceptions, can be accomplished by a change in elevation or perspective.

The Mineral Element

"Each person needs to remember the knowledge stored in one's bones … Mineral is what provides the basic building blocks for life—memory and communication. Every gene is encoded with mineral memory in order for it to evolve in a particular pattern, and fulfill a particular purpose" (*Water Wisdom*, by Mbyiu K. I. Chui).

The energy manifesting within the Mineral element or spirit relates to memories and documenting the passage of time and one's life experiences and relationships. It serves to bridge the gap between past and present and speaks to the ability of the Mineral spirit to relay memories, either vocally or in writing, in a way that interconnects. Mineral energy also has the ability to interact with the energy level of the spirit within a person. Mineral energy can act as a gauge in the case of one's sixth sense being stimulated by an event, or to strengthen or disperse the energy of a person by using stones and crystals to balance their chakras.

For rituals, it is good to keep a variety of stones, crystals, and shells energized for use in the ritual process or for including in talisman or medicine bags. They may also be placed around a room when cleansing and to balance the energy in a space. The dust of stones can be placed in water to energize the water for ritual use.

Chapter 5

SPIRITUAL TOOLS

The use of spiritual tools speaks to our need to feed into the powers of nature and the elements to enhance and elevate our energy in the spiritual realm and the realm of our ancestors. They are not mandatory or even necessary, but if needed, like any other tool, they are available and energetically willing to be of assistance in spiritual work. Spiritual tools will come to you in a variety of ways; some you will find, and others will be given to you. Many times, if we look around us, we will be surprised at the spiritual tools we already have. Items that were handed down are the best, regardless of what they were used for. But any item that you claim as a spiritual tool must be imbued with your energy and spirit.

Oils

The study of aroma therapy is very extensive. The influence of scent on the body's energy centers and on the mind, how it is interpreted and what it is able to manifest, is what we want to focus on. I like to group my oils in categories of hot (up), cold (down), warm (inside), and cool (outside). Whether I want to feel activated, calm, introverted, or extraverted dictates where I start.

When using an oil for the first time, it is important to analyze the impact on the mind, and hence, the body, so I recommend using one oil at a time for a day. As you practice blending oils, think of building layer on top of layer of scents, each holding a purpose or intent individually, and becoming a whole scent with a purpose or intent of its own. The focal scent is in the middle and should always retain its focal status. The base scent is underneath (that can be heightened with heat), and the high scent that adds the desired twist or shock (that usually dissipates and blends into the whole) is on top.

There are many resources for information on blending oils and which aspect of the body and mind they affect, and many oils have similar properties and uses. In choosing which oil to use for a specific purpose, you should consider whether the oil is readily available to you, if it is in its pure and natural state for a higher frequency, any negative physical side effects, and whether the scent is compatible with the other scents selected. At least one of the oils should focus on the energetic effects you want to manifest, and another on the psychological effects. The end result should have a spiritual quality that will transport (if not transform) a person's thoughts and actions to a higher level of vibration, to uplift their Divine selves.

Crystals/Stones

Rocks, stones, shells, bones, and salts are thought to be inanimate objects. However, molecular activity inherent in all matter and that produces a measurable level of vibration verifies that this is not true. The mineral's ability to attract matter to itself, thereby engaging in the divine task of growth, is an indicator that all minerals (including decaying bone) are animate and alive. The following quote from *Water Wisdom* elaborates on this concept: "Mineral spirits have a responsibility to the rocks, and can learn much from listening and allowing them to speak to them." It is best to use rocks and gemstones that are in their natural state, undrilled, uncut, and unpolished. Select rocks from places that carry a strong energy, such as a vortex or a place that is special to you.

Rocks—

Rocks are classified according to their origin, composition, and method of formation: igneous (from within the earth), sedimentary (from the earth's crust), and metamorphic (combinations of rocks under extreme pressure). Rocks also have the property to repel or absorb heat. Rocks that repel heat (sedimentary and metamorphic) can be used in a mineral ritual by enveloping the person in stone—either by forming a circle of rocks and sitting the person inside the circle or by sitting in a cave of rocks. This type of mineral ritual is used in cases where a person is seeking their purpose or attempting to remember something. Rocks that absorb heat (igneous) are used in a form of deep-tissue massage to relax the body and stimulate the flow of blood and energy throughout the body. Rocks can be energized by using other elements— water running over rock will "help their creative juices flow more freely," fire in the form of a tea-light candle placed on a rock will "help them become more visible in their purpose." This may also explain the importance of heating divining shells to energize them.

Gemstones—

Gemstones are a part of the metamorphic classification of stones. Stones such as the pearl and amber are made from animal and mineral deposits. Precious and semiprecious gemstones are classified as quartz, beryl, or crystal, or a combination. Gemstones can be used in several ways: made into jewelry to be worn by a Diviner and client, a stone to carry on your person either for a specific reason or in combination with other stones, or used to energize water that will be used in healing practices. The beryl family of stones—emerald, aquamarine, hessonite, red beryl—is best used for divining because they enhance one's creative/intuitive energies.

Shells and Bones—

Shells come from the sea and carry a water energy that relates to intuitive wisdom. Cowrie and conch shells are commonly used for divination in many Aboriginal cultures. Bones from animals are also used in divination, and in a powder state can be added to other materials to make medicine for inner healing (white) and outer cleansing (black).

Salts—

Salt, also a product of the sea, carries the aspect of water energy that relates to cleansing. In its natural state or dissolved in water, salt is used to cleanse undesirable energy from crystals and other divination tools, and in the absence of ash, to cleanse spaces.

Statues/Masks

It was difficult for me to start this section because statues have always been important to me. I just didn't know why. Over the years, I accumulated several pieces that resonated strongly with me at first sight. Whether it's ancient from one of the shrines in Africa, or newly made (and aged) by skilled artisans, it's all in the intent with which it was made, putting your energy into it to enliven it, keeping it energized with oils and smoke, and using them.

I am floored every year to see the amount of medicine-laden statues that come out of the shrines of Africa. These are powerful spiritual tools that were created for a purpose, and before we arbitrarily bring them into our homes, we need to know what that purpose was, where the piece is from, and whether it was acquired righteously. When I was in Senegal, I purchased several pieces, one from an artisan, and one from a shop owner who I suspected was also a traditionalist/spiritualist. I was able to sit down over tea and not only negotiate a price but acquire information on the purpose and any medicine that might be left.

One must sit with a statue and listen to it, feel its presence in the space. Touch the statue, run your hands over it, and feel every mark on it. Study the mask or statute, always listening, being in tune with yourself and any affect the statue has on you. As you continue listening to your statue/mask, it may ask for some type of decoration. You usually see these things in a dream state, or you may look at the statue/mask and see it decorated. The energy that you put into your statue/mask relates to the energy you get back.

Staffs/Wands

When I make a staff for a client, I always take it for a walk in a high energy place (usually around water) and talk to it. I always tell it, "You may be called on to transform … make me proud!" I learned the skill of staff making from Grand Master Sekou and learned a little about wands from my travels. These are not just symbols of status, but tools that can be imbued with words and symbols of power (hekau), medicine, gemstones, and other items that have been energized with a specific intent for a specific purpose. When we look at the construction of a staff, we must first look at the wood, which brings me to a story.

I was visiting a sacred place in South Carolina known as Beulah Land. I had gone with the intention of performing a nature ritual, so I brought several warm weather plants that I had started at home; mango, avocado, and pineapple plants. Grand Master Sekou and I had just met, and he told me about the staffs he had made while in the city but that he didn't have one of his own. On my last day at Beulah Land with one plant left, the avocado plant, I went off into the woods to find a suitable home for it to flourish.

From what I knew about avocado trees, I stumbled upon a ravine with a lot of fallen trees but still pretty thick, and decided that somewhere along the edge would be best. After planting the tree, I sat down on a huge log that had literally fallen across the ravine. It was a very peaceful place, and the thought came to me to find a limb for my teacher to make a staff for himself. I climbed down from the log and walked up and down the ravine, kicking over branches and rocks, picking up limbs and putting them back. Finally, I was ready to give up. I told myself that I didn't know what I was even looking for, what type of wood, what shape, what size would make a good staff. There were so many factors to consider, I started to feel lightheaded. I sat for a few more minutes before preparing myself to jump down off the log and suddenly, that clear, concise voice spoke to me again. It said, "No, you can't leave; you brought something special to this place, now you must take something back. It's your right; that's how things are done." I said thank you and jumped down.

I began looking again. This time I knew I didn't have the vaguest idea what I was looking for, but I knew that I would find it. Suddenly, I saw a tree limb that looked dead, but it had a green fernlike plant growing out from it. I reached down to lift it up, but it wouldn't budge. I followed down the length of the limb and saw that there was a huge rock and a lot of leaves sitting on the end, so I pushed the rock off and lifted the limb. It was huge, about eight feet tall or more, and thick. I brushed it off, looked it over, and said a prayer of thanks. Thanks for the foresight to hold the ritual, thanks for the blessing of the limb, and thanks for the power of Spirit to teach me about the spiritual way. We cleansed, energized, and dressed the staff together. When we walk with that staff, needless to say, it has a powerful impact on people and makes a statement wherever it goes. The magic with which it was imbued continues to manifest miracles and blessings in our lives.

Jewelry

It's timely for the topic of jewelry to come up since I recently obtained eight strands of ruby bracelets which I energized in the name of the Goddess Sekhmet and wore for a first-time consultation. When I sat down in the room, I immediately went into trance. Needless to say, the gathering was quite revealing, and we were able to cut to the chase painlessly. I found that I was able to go into trance quickly and effortlessly with a strong lucidity. I have jewelry that I wear every day. Each has a special meaning for me, and I have jewelry that I only use in doing spiritual work. Both should be cleared and energized with a specific intent. As tools, jewelry will come to you in many unexpected ways. One should not be concerned about that. It's about being open hearted and in flow with Spirit to receive.

Clothing

Everything a spiritualist puts on their physical body should be as natural as possible. Be it their oils, jewelry, or clothing, it should be in its natural state to ensure the unobstructed flow of energy and oxygenation of the body on a cellular level. Fabrics should be used that are breathable and preferably made of a sustainable plant by-product. Each person must decide how much energy or focus they will put into their clothing. Many spiritualists wear elaborate garments, believing that it uplifts their energy level. Many spiritualists will only wear specific colors. I have been directed by Spirit to wear red linen, and although I have not begun that experience, no doubt it will aid my work. Like everything else, clothing should be energized, either the raw cloth or the finished garment. I have found in the conduct of rituals, certain clothing works better, or Spirit may move me to wear specific garments. It has always been a case of function over form.

Sound

Sound therapy as a healing tool is critical in the transformation process. Whether one uses recorded music, bells,
drums or some other instrument, sound is an ethereal energy that easily interacts with other energy, especially human energy. Sound transforms, and there have been many
extensive studies on how hekau (words of power) has a
transformative effect on water, and how it interacts with
the human body. With the assistance of biofeedback technology, it has been shown that the sound "ung" resonates
in and energizes the third eye chakra. When performing the
cobra breath, one is instructed to make a "hissing" sound
when you exhale. When the sound is moderated in intensity
and duration, it creates a vibration that reverberates in the
material and spiritual realm.

Incense

I have heard incense described as the sweet and savory scent
pleasing to the gods. When burning incense, it is important
to select one with purpose that has been energized with your
intent. Incense is available in a number of forms: stick, cone,
loose for coals, or diffuser with oil. Whatever the form, it is
the incense that creates an overall energy in your space. In
clearing a space, it is good as a last measure to burn incense
in the four corners to infuse the scent and the fire elements.
One's sacred or ritual space should be "smoked out" periodically to maintain the desired energy level.

Candles

This is one spiritual tool that has so many uses, it's a good idea to purchase them in bulk or have the ability to make your own. If you live in a cold or overcast environment, candles replicate the energy of fire in a very contained state. The single flame can be just as powerful as the sun. Meditating on a single flame will take you into trance and serve the same purpose as a full outdoor fire ritual. In the same way as burning something transforms it and gives it new energy, a lit candle, especially a seven-day candle, will generate a lot of energy and transform a situation when imbued with a focused intent. Your candles should always be energized and blessed with an oil. When giving a candle to someone for spiritual purposes, decorating it with power symbols and hekau is helpful to increase their energy and help them maintain the focus. When using fire indoors, it is important to use safety measures like placing the candle in or next to a bowl of water. When extinguishing a candle, I prefer not blowing out the flame, but covering the flame, or using wet fingers.

Talismans

Talismans are objects that are imbued with one's energy, and can be used to provide protection for the carrier or wearer. Talismans can also be made for a group with a common intent/purpose, and can be made by a spiritualist on their behalf and placed on a common altar or sacred space. A talisman is made using a variety of herbs, symbols of power and strength, oils, "medicine," and coins. These items are wrapped in a cloth or placed in a bag that is then energized. The most powerful talisman is imbued with the maker or wearer's bodily fluid and covered again. It can be worn or carried, buried in ash or in the ground, or placed on an altar or sacred space after the final adorning.

Feathers

I was led by a native spirit to include this category, and as I began writing this, it dawned on me … how could I have left this tool out when I use it all the time? The feathers came to us through Spirit, and by expressing my desire and intent, being consistent with our work, and being thankful for the small things. Grand Master Sekou and I were out performing our daily ritual work on a small island off the coastline of downtown Detroit. We were there giving offerings in the form of food for the animals and making offerings to the river. I had spoken about our need for feathers and set the intent in my mind earlier that day to find a white feather.

As I sat in the car waiting for Grand Master Sekou to return, I noticed a white feather lying on the ground. As I went to pick it up and wave it in excitement, I noticed a family of swans in the lake across the road were swimming toward the shore. Well, I knew that I had to go over and feed the swans to give thanks for the gift of the feather. I crossed the street, looking at the swans to make eye contact with the male who could be quite aggressive if not approached properly. I began to throw down bread crumbs, and the whole family got out of the water and surrounded me. Even the male came up to me and snatched at a piece of bread in my hand. It was all quite strange. As the swans retreated to the water, the male stopped, turned around with wings raised, and sqawked at me. I looked over at Grand Master Sekou, who was equally amazed.

As the family swam off and I stood up, I looked down on

the ground, only to realize that I was standing surrounded by numerous geese feathers. I called Grand Master Sekou over, he had not noticed the feathers either, but that day we picked up almost 100 beautiful feathers. I stumbled upon the remains of the bird that had been sacrificed and said a prayer of thanks and assurance that the feathers would be used properly. We spent weeks cleansing and energizing the feathers, and they have been a powerful tool for energetic wrapping and sweeping work.

A single feather is powerful because it carries the energy of the animal from which it comes. The feather of a high-flying bird that soars into the heavens can be effectively used to direct energy in the form of smoke or spirit into the heavens since the bird has been there and is familiar with that realm. Feathers from water birds I find are excellent for the sweeping process when doing house cleansings. Only highly energized feathers should be used for sweeping an individual of negative energy. I love to use water bird feathers, like from ducks and geese; but to seal the person, I use swan feathers in a circular motion around the person. Precious feathers should be willingly given by the animal or found already separated from the bird. Feathers should be washed thoroughly, salted or ashed, talked to, stroked, oiled, sunned, smoked, and generally loved. They're like a plant or water; they respond to your energy and the energy around it.

Chapter 6

MAGIC

Magic is the ability to release the higher Spirit within one's self to manifest changes in yourself and your environment. It is through performing acts of ritual that one increases his or her ability to go into a trance state where the higher Spirit is allowed to function without interference from the mind or ego. One's ability to perform magic is also related to one's intent for entering into the state of trance and should always be related to a positive outcome and for the benefit of self and others. This is an important point. Through the exercise of Divine wisdom, spiritual power is manifest for the benefit of all, not for one's benefit alone. Many spiritualists and ritualists have told me that they have a problem using their magic on their own behalf, or that their magic works for others but not for them. It is important to find that balance, because if you don't ask for yourself, or only ask for yourself, you definitely won't receive. Remember the points outlined in Chapter 2 in the Environment section—Balance!

Exercising these energies should also be beneficial to all living entities and the environment, and the results should be positive. Therefore, magic is not used against anyone or anything, but to strengthen or uplift the person for whom magic is performed. It should not be used to fight against anything, but to shield or guide the one in need. This is the difference between what Western society terms as "black magic" and "white magic." Even the uses of such terms are not true descriptions. The former is used against someone or something, and the latter is used to the benefit of someone or something. Whatever reason for performing acts of magic and ritual, one must be prepared to take responsibility for the outcome, whether beneficial or not.

Trance and Transformation

The key to performing magic is the ability to go into a trance state. It is in this state of trance that one has the ability to transform; either their behavior, their knowledge or understanding, or their experience. The trance state can be entered into through consistent practice of meditation and breathing exercises, conditioning the body to move and control one's internal energy, and by having a clear intent.

In the Kemetic teachings, according to the Paut Neteru (11 Laws of God), the energy related to trance and transformation is Auset (Isis). It was through going into trance that she was able to locate the hidden body of her husband Ausar (Osiris) on two occasions. Through her ability to transform, she was able to reunite the severed parts of her husband and conceive a child, Heru (Horus), who fought his uncle Set to regain the status of his father. Visualizing Auset while in meditation is another tool to assist in entering the trance state. Once a clear image of her figure is obtained, one should substitute their face for hers, to visualize oneself in her image and possessing her powers to enter into trance and transform. Once the trance state has been realized, one has the ability to realize their intent, with or without the assistance of another energy or Spirit, and to travel to other planes of existence and other dimensions.

Shields and Connecting with Higher Energies

Putting up one's shields is a process of connecting with familiar spirit guides and/or your ancestors as a protection when going into trance. Energizing your shields is a process of connecting with sun, earth, and other universal energies. Both are important when interacting in the spiritual realm to assist others, when travelling on other planes of existence and in other dimensions, or when opening yourself up in a low-energy environment or around people with low energy.

Another component of performing magic and some rituals is infusing your energy into spiritual tools, either through your saliva, hair, breath, or some other personal item. Shields help to protect you in the event that the spiritual tool is not used as intended, or falls into the hands of someone who is not benevolent to your intent. This practice will heighten and protect your energy and the energy or intent of the client or recipient. It is important for practitioners to keep their energies high and their shields up when performing energetic work on others so that their energy is not drained. This is especially true for ritualists/spiritualists working with people who are ill or who have a lot of trauma that they are working through.

The act of connecting with Spirits can move into the realm of spiritual possession. In European cultures, this is considered a bad thing. In aboriginal cultures, it is considered a positive confirmation of oneness with Spirit that opens the door for the practitioner to have a relationship with a particular or group of Spirits for protection and guidance. When this happens, a person must sacrifice something to receive the higher energy, such as a commitment to give up something, or to walk away from a situation, or to honor the Spirit by being obedient and performing ritual in their or its name. This maintains spiritual balance and should not be looked at as a burden, but rather an honor.

Making Sacrifice

In many Aboriginal cultures, animal sacrifice and blood rituals are performed, but this should not be looked upon as a forced deed, and one must use his or her common sense when making sacrifice. At one point, I was tested by a Spirit and told to sacrifice my relationship with someone in my family to obtain higher spiritual gifts and success in life. I respectfully refused, but as I remained faithful in my work, I was blessed in many ways.

I have participated in several sacrifice rituals, being sprayed with the blood, and having items energized with the blood. It is taking something ancient and full of life and using that life energy to elevate oneself. It is a humbling experience and should be undertaken in total humility and gratitude for the being that gives up its life.

One must be prepared to balance out this type of sacrifice with a free-willed spreading of that energy, and the power received, to others in word or deed. There are many processes that are associated with the sacrifice; eating the meat of the sacrificed animal, pulverizing the bones for medicine, and in some cases, drinking of the blood in a mixture. In the book *Conversations with Ogotemmeli, An Introduction to Dogon Religious Ideas* by Marcel Griaule, the elder Ogotemmeli explains the cyclical process of the energetic flow that occurs. The energy that flows between the sacrificed and the sacrificer, that is transmitted to the partakers of the remains, who transmit the energy out to the community as a whole through words and deeds. The energy is then released back to the spiritual realm and can be called to action as needed. One must be aware of who performs such sacrifices and whether their intent is clear and benevolent, and that one's intent is clear and benevolent in requesting the sacrifice, not just for self, but for all.

Energizing Spiritual Tools

An important function of magic is to energize one's tools. This will ensure that the spirits that assist you in your work have a place to reside, and that your and their energy can be dispersed out into the universe through the use of that energized tool. Injecting and conducting spiritual energy through an object will magnify the intent. You may construct an object that represents the person or their intent, and you may write hekau on an object. You might use something that they already have, or an object that you have energized and set aside for later use.

During my group excursion into Senegal, we met with a spiritual leader in the countryside where the land was very sandy. Inside of the meeting room, in the middle of the floor was a rock, about the size of a football, with no exceptional characteristics to speak of. After much wondering, we asked the spiritual leader the purpose of the rock in the middle of the room, and he related the following story, which I will paraphrase. When the group first moved out into the countryside, before any water wells were dug, water was very scarce. When it came time to perform their prayers, they needed to wash their hands and feet. With water being so scarce, the men came to the spiritual leader and asked how they would wash before prayer, and the spiritual leader went into prayer to seek a solution. He was told that if there was not enough water, to use sand to wash before prayer, and if there was no sand, to use a rock. The most important thing was to perform the prayers at the appointed times. So they keep a rock in the middle of the room to remind them that it is not the method that is important, but the intent, and that it was more important to keep prayer time even though the conditions might not be perfect. Well, at least that's what I got out of the story, and as I reflected on the situation and on times when I didn't have everything perfect. Spirit always says, be clear in your intent and improvise!

The magic comes into play by being able to energize the rock to project your intent, either collectively or individually. Whatever form your spiritual tools take, it is important to care for them and periodically reenergize them. The energizing process also depends on what is available, but the main steps include cleansing to clear old energy, energizing with intent, and maintenance. Initially, it is important to clean the object. This may be as simple as washing the object with a natural mild soap, and/or letting the object soak in water for several days, or a more complex task of removing a layer or finish using sandpaper. Energizing the object can include burying the object in salt, letting it sit in direct sunlight, then rubbing scented oil or some personal fluid on the object to give it energy and a connection with your energy.

The maintenance step depends on the object itself and may include oil to nourish wood or keep metal from rusting and/ or smoke to infuse the object with renewed life.

Altars and Personal Space

My mentor Baba Ishangi once said regarding altars, keep it simple. By simple he explained that all you needed was a table, a table covering, a candle, a glass of water, a symbol of nature, and an item (book, picture) that reflected your spiritual path. There are several types of altars or shrines: ancestral, familial, and personal. Whatever the purpose, it is more important to maintain the altar on a regular basis and keep it clear of clutter and dust. It is where you go to make prayer or meditate, and where you call on Spirit. You know that you have a powerful altar when you're away from it and can close your eyes and see everything on the altar and can feel the energy of the altar.

Wherever you set up your altar is your personal space. Many people suggest finding your personal space first, and then setting up your altar, but with today's urban lifestyle and living conditions, you may only be able to secure a space for your altar with barely three feet in front of it. As the mother of three, I had to set parameters with my children regarding my altar space that, out of necessity, was accessible to them. They could come and sit with me if they remained still, or they would be given a task, but they soon acclimated themselves to the fact that when Mommy is in meditation or at the altar, they must not disturb her. That is not to say that they had to be quiet outside of the space, it was my responsibility to remain focused in my meditation regardless of what was going on around me.

Your altar is your place of refuge and retreat, and if properly energized, it can be a source of strength. Develop a personal bond with your altar and the tools you place there, knowing that when you set up an altar, you are calling Spirit into that space to honor them with the items (especially sacrifices) you place on it. The Dogon elder Ogotemmeli explains it thusly, "The altar gives something to a man, and a part of what he has received he passes on to others ... A small part of the sacrifice is for oneself, but the rest is for others. The forces released enter into the man, pass through him and out again, and so it is for all ... The Word (Nummo) is for everyone in this world; it must come and go and be interchanged, for it is good to give and to receive the forces of life." Many nights I fall asleep in front of my altar and have the most profound dreams that I readily share with others.

Healing Stones

Rocks and stones should be bathed before they are used to clear them of any processes and handling they may have incurred. They can then be purified by allowing them to sit in a glass container of salt, then rinsed and placed in a container of water that has been infused with words of power that relate to how the rock or stone will be used. Hold the container close to your mouth when you speak and set the container on an altar or shrine for several days before use. Rocks and stones can also be purified by setting them in a place where they will get direct exposure to sunlight for several days. Lastly, rocks and stones can also be buried in the earth for a number of days for purification. However, choose a burying place that has a strong energy. Shells and bones are purified using a variety of formulas: soaked in heated MSG and shea butter, or milk and alcohol. Those are just two formulas that can be used.

I keep a large piece of rose quartz near my computer to keep my thoughts clear while working on the computer. When I am divining a person, I ask them to hold a piece of stone, either clear quartz to energize them, rose to diffuse anger or bad feelings, amethyst to help work through the details to see the bigger picture, aventurine to stimulate creative thinking, or citrine to get them energized. Labradorite and watermelon tourmaline (bicolor) are excellent stones to carry to bring balance to the wearer, and emeralds are considered the Diviner's stone for its ability to open the conscience and increase imagination. A rock salt lamp is a critical tool to neutralize one's environment by releasing ionic energy, and there are claims of a wide range of health benefits, one of which is to improve one's quality of sleep, and thereby, their dream state. I recently acquired a large black tourmaline to clear away negative spirits in our environment and to promote healing in clients. Heated chakra stones are very powerful and can be used in a variety of ways to stimulate and energize the holder or wearer.

FINAL REMARKS

As a ritualist practicing in an urban setting, I have found that what some might interpret as a disadvantage has truly been a blessing. It has made me expand my creative side in the most basic ways. I have found a quiet, peaceful place within myself, in the midst of the insanity. I give thanks and praises every morning and every evening.

I encourage you to take a similar journey of self-discovery, seeing your past from a myriad of perspectives, evaluating your present self and relationships, and visualizing your transformed future self. Hear your song, tell your story, hold the light for the upliftment of all. The rewards are astonishing!

Be kind to yourself, knowing that you are a child of the universe, loved and cherished by spirit, and one with all.

Peace and Love

Ashe, Ashe, Ashe O

APPENDIX A

Postures

Let's begin in a standing posture—

1. Feet together, toes and heels touching
2. Bend knees slightly
3. Pelvic relaxed and tucked slightly forward
4. Chest out
5. Shoulders down and back
6. Head up, and eyes straight-ahead

If you feel comfortable, try to maintain this standing posture. If it is putting too much strain on any part of the body, feel free to sit with the lower back supported. Maintain the chest out, shoulders down and back, and head up with eyes straight-ahead. Most importantly, relax and breath!

Breathing Exercises

The breath is the vehicle that transports the vital energy that flows through every organ of the body via the bloodstream and through the energy centers via the meridians. We have been conditioned to breathe from the chest area, but that limits the breath and chokes off the vital energy from reaching the full body. The correct way to breathe through the entire body is—

1. Assume the standing posture
2. Hold your hand on your lower abdomen and exhale all the air from the body until you can feel your lower abdomen tighten.
3. Inhale slowly through the nose and into the lower abdomen, relaxing the stomach and the chest, and allowing them to expand.
4. Without holding the breath, begin exhaling all of the air from your chest, then stomach, then lower abdomen until the lower abdomen feels tight.
5. Without holding the breath, begin inhaling again, focusing the mind on where you want the breath to go.
6. Exhale when the breath reaches the top of the chest, again focusing the mind on where you want the breath to go.

The next step is to develop a series of breath exercises that you can use to enhance your meditation. Practice 1-minute drills to help expand your lung capacity and breath control:

1. Inhale for 1 minute
2. Exhale for 1 minute
3. Inhale and hold breath in for 1 minute
4. Exhale and hold breath out for 1 minute.

This exercise will help you achieve the "Golden Breath" used in Kemet. Practice while seated, cross your legs or sit in a lotus position, or lying down; and use a mudra (hand posture) that will lock the energy as there is a tendency to become light-headed in the beginning.

1. Inhale for 10 seconds, hold breath for 5 seconds, and exhale for 15 seconds. Repeat seven times.
2. Inhale for 15 seconds, hold breath for 5 seconds, and exhale for 20 seconds. Repeat five times.
3. Inhale for 20 seconds, hold breath for 5 seconds, and exhale for 25 seconds. Repeat three times.
4. Inhale for 25 seconds, hold breath for 5 seconds, and exhale for 30 seconds. This is the Golden Breath and should be repeated as many times as possible.

The following pattern should be used with the hekau that follows, and should be practiced in stages, first focusing on the breath only, next adding the locks, lastly with alternating nostrils.

1. Begin the breath count for the inhale, hold, and exhale at four counts.
2. The perineum lock consists of squeezing the perineum muscle located between the vagina/scrotum and the anal muscles. It is the muscle that is contracted when you attempt to cut off your urine flow.
3. The abdomen lift is best accomplished when the abdomen is emptied of air so that the abdominal muscle can be lifted toward the chest.

Repeat the breath four times, then six times, then eight times, always making sure that you are relaxed through the entire cycle before moving to the next level. Also, extend the breath count to six counts, then eight counts and so on.

Add the alternating nostril technique as follows:

1. Close off the right nostril with your thumb and inhale through the left nostril.
2. Hold the breath and close off both nostrils using your thumb on the right side and your middle finger on the left nostril.
3. Open the left nostril to exhale, and close off both nostrils during the last hold.
4. Open the left nostril to inhale and continue the breathing rotation, always beginning the new rotation inhaling in the nostril that you last exhaled from.

By practicing the posture and breathing exercises, you will dramatically increase your energy level and begin the healing process. Practice at every opportunity throughout the day. No matter where you are, you can correct your posture and practice a breathing technique. The purpose is to feel energy flowing through your body with every inhale, hold, and exhale. Always remain relaxed.

Physical Exercises

A good morning exercise will energize and flex various parts of the body quickly and efficiently. One such exercise is this form of The Five Irishes:

1. Stand in the standing posture with feet together and and arms at your sides. Inhale, raising arms straight up the side (using your shoulders) and overhead with palms coming together. Squeeze your hands and entire body for 2–3 seconds and release by exhaling and lowering arms to sides. Repeat three times, making

sure that the shoulders remain relaxed, arms are pulled back to your ears, and your breath is flowing.

2. Inhale, raising arms straight up the side with the back of the hands coming together. Squeeze your hands and entire body for 2–3 seconds and release by exhaling and lowering arms to the sides. Repeat three times.

3. Inhale, arms straight up, and grasp thumbs and pull. Exhale bending the upper torso at the hips to the left side and pushing hips to the right, allowing the arms to follow; inhale the body and arms straight up and exhale releasing thumbs and lowering arms to the side. Repeat the exercise bending the upper torso and extended arms to the right side from the hip and pushing the hips to the left. Repeat the entire exercise three times.

4. Inhale, hands behind back, grasping thumbs and pull. Step straight out with the right leg. Exhale, bending over at the hips until the abdomen touches upper thigh and raising your arms behind you. Inhale body straight up and release thumbs and step your right foot back. Repeat on the left side. Repeat the entire exercise three times.

5. Inhale, arms straight up and bend back; exhale while raising the body up and bending forward from the hips until the back is flat and your arms straight out. Repeat three times and allow the arms and upper torso to drop on the last forward bend, then roll the upper torso up to the standing posture.

Hekau

The most effective words of power that I have used were taught to me by my yoga Master Kwesi Karamoko, and are as follows:

Aung, Grang, Gring, Graung

They are sounds with no meaning, but hold the purpose of creating a vibration first in the mouth, then in the chakras, and lastly, throughout the body. I have had experiences where I believe intoning these words vibrates outside of the body at a level that is detected by nature. Each letter should be enunciated. The words are intoned consciously at first until you reach the point where the words ring in your spirit, like a song that you hear in the morning that continues to ring in your head for the rest of the day. They can be used with the four-count breathing pattern previously outlined.

APPENDIX B

Rituals

The most important ritual you can perform is the ancestral feeding. This ritual honors our memories and celebrates our continued relationship with our ancestors.

When you are cooking a meal, and you realize that this was one of your ancestor's favorite foods and/or drink, before anyone tastes the food, prepare a plate for the ancestor. Meditate on that spirit and your relationship while you prepare the plate (made out of a natural material). Place the plate on your altar along with a photo or possession that belonged to the ancestor or that represents something the ancestor loved doing. Light a red or white (or both) candle next to the food and drink (a glass of water is a good substitute). When I feed my ancestors, I will sit at the altar and commune with them, and partake in one of the items on the altar (a cigar or drink). After three or so days, I will take the food outdoors and offer it to a tree, giving thanks to the spirit of my ancestor and asking the tree, and every being that feeds on the tree, to bless the offering. Over the years, my neighbors have become accustomed to this scene. I will walk around the tree three times counterclockwise, touching it or stopping to hug it.

I have always included my children in this ritual and am very pleased that my youngest daughter, at the age of 20, performed her first ancestral feeding ritual without even telling me until she finished.

Spiritual Baths

Spiritual baths as ritual have several components: 1) the gathering of the tools to be used and the blessing and energizing of each, 2) the prayer calling forth the spirits and making the request, 3) the bath and meditation, 4) the closing prayer giving thanks. These are several spiritual baths taught to me by my mentor Baba Ishangi which are very powerful.

Kra Da (Soul's Day)—This ritual is performed to celebrate the day of the week on which one was born. It is designed to celebrate the three stages of your life: past, present, and future; and to give you an opportunity to give thanks to Divine Spirit and your ancestors, and to make requests specifically for yourself.

You will need some spiritual bath oil or what is commonly known as "Florida Water," a natural soap (African black soap), a bucket of water that you can stand in and lift, a red candle, and a bath towel that is used for rituals only.

Early in the morning, pour a generous amount of spiritual bath oil in the bucket of water. Light your candle(s) and open the ritual with prayer. Stand in the bucket continuing the prayer and soap up the towel using the prepared water formula. As you wash yourself from head to toe, give thanks for the past you. Lift the bucket and pour a small amount over your body to rinse off. Soap up the towel again and wash yourself, giving thanks for the present you, and rinse again. The third time you wash, give thanks for your future self, and to rinse, pour the water over your head first, then over the rest of your body. Pat yourself dry and cover yourself in fragrance-free talc powder. If possible, go straight to your altar and make your request, leaving the candle lit until it goes out on its own; otherwise, dress in light-colored clothing first. Eat light foods, and take it easy for the day. If you meet someone else born on the same day, give them something.

New Moon—This ritual is performed on the day of the new moon to celebrate new beginnings and renewed spirit and commitment.

You will need three containers to hold two hair wash solutions and a conditioner solution that will rinse easily. A fourth solution consists of spring water, spiritual bath oil, and a drop of honey about the size of a nickel. You also need a white candle and a natural cup to dip in the fourth solution and pour over the hair.

Light the candle and begin by washing your hair with the first solution and rinsing with clean water, using the same process to rinse as you used to wash. Repeat with the second wash and rinse. On the third wash, with the conditioning solution, do not rinse the hair with clean water; instead, use the forth solution. Dip the natural cup in the solution and pour it over your head while honoring the spirits and the ancestors. Think about the past 30 days and the benefits you have gained. Do not rinse out the forth solution. Pat your body dry with a towel, and dry your hair naturally, if possible. Go directly to your altar to give thanks and meditate on your requests for the next 30 days. Allow the candle to burn out on its own.

You may choose to write your requests as part of the ritual. To energize your written request, use a red pen and write on natural or parchment paper. Energize it with your energy and fold it as you pray to spirit. You can walk with the paper in your shoe; bundle it with incense and other energized items and take it to the river or bury it, burn it and use the ash, or any combination of the above.

APPENDIX C

Oil Blends

It is important to use essential oils that are organic or pure grade. You can use a base oil such as olive, grape-seed, or jojoba oil, and build the scent from there. Use the heavier tones and build to the lighter ones. You can always go back and reinforce the base if needed. Allow the blends to sit on your altar for several days, blending them each day by rolling the bottle in your hands, then take the top off and breathe your intent for the oil into the bottle. If you feel that the oil is not blending well, place the bottle in a pan of hot water for several minutes. I am including a sampling of blends that relate to the Kemetic Neteru:

Ra (fire)—Frankincense, orange, cinnamon

Tehuti (wisdom)—Sage, cedarwood, cinnamon, bay, rosemary, lavender

Auset (trance)—Myrrh, sandalwood, frankincense, rose, oud/musk

Ausar (discernment)—Cedarwood, pine, myrrh,

patchouli, benzoin

Crystals and Stones

Information on the relationship between stones, elements, chakras, and astrology can be found in the following publications: "Opening to Spirit" by Caroline Shola Arewa; "Rainbow of Chakra Centers—Body-Mind Connections" by Inner Light Resources' Rainbow Cards Charts Series; and "Chakra Centers" and "Astrology" Sacred Wisdom Charts by Helion Publishing. In summary, the three top stones that relate to the five elements are:

Earth—Root Chakra—Ruby, garnet, hematite

Water—Sacral Chakra—Coral, carnelian, moonstone

Fire—Solar Plexus Chakra—Citrine, amber, golden topaz

Nature—Heart Chakra—Green tourmaline, emerald, green jade

Mineral—Throat Chakra—Blue lace agate, aquamarine, turquoise

For the elements of Light (Third Eye Chakra) and Spirit (Crown Chakra), lapis lazuli and diamond are related respectively.

Candles

Lighting one's space with candles is like lighting your life. The use of candles and your belief system dictates the color that is used for a particular purpose. Colors can be chosen to relate to the elements, to a deity or spirit, or simply to honor a day of the week. I would like to give a general description of the energies that different colors evoke:

Red—giving honor to the ancestors and to one's "kra da" (also called one's soul day, the day of the week that you were born)

White—a general color that can be used in conjunction with other colors or to purify

Green—change; for those far away from you; prosperity

Yellow—when cleansing a space, for support; also prosperity

Blue—increase intuitive powers; clearing; honor indigo spirit

Brown—when a favorable decision is being sought

Pink—uplift a love; peaceful; reconciling energy

You may notice that I did not include Black. Although it is a blending of all colors, it also has an attraction to spirits that I am not familiar with.

REFERENCES AND RECOMMENDED READINGS

Afrika, Llaila O. 2009. *Melanin, What Makes Black People Black!* Seaburn Publishing, Long Island City.

Amen, Ra Un Nefer. 2008. *Metu Neter: The Key To Miracles*, Vol. 3. Khamit Media Trans Visions, Inc., Brooklyn.

Ani (Richards), Dr. Dona Marimba. 1980. *Let The Circle Be Unbroken*. Red Sea Press, Inc., New Jersey.

Arewa, Caroline Shola. 1998. *Opening to Spirit*. Thorsons, London.

ben-Jochannan, Dr. Yosef A. A. 1972. *Black Man of the Nile and His Family*. Alkebu-lan Books and Education Materials Association, New York.

Bynum, Dr. Edward Bruce, Editor; Dr. Ann C. Brown, Dr. Richard D. King, and Dr. T. Owens Moore. *Why Darkness Matters: The Power of Melanin in the Brain,* Compilation.

African American Images.

Chandler, Wayne. 1999. *Ancient Futures: The Teachings and Prophetic Wisdom of the Seven Hermetic Laws*. Black Classic Press.

Clarke, Dr. John Henrik. *History of Violence in Western Society*. DVD.

Diop, Cheikh Anta. 1955. *The African Origin of Civilization: Myth or Reality*. Présence Africaine, Paris.

Griaule, Marcel. 1965. *Conversations with Ogotemmeli*. International African Institute London.

James, George G. M. 1954. *Stolen Legacy*. African American Images.

Pookram, Dr. Jewel. 2003. *Vitamins and Minerals From A To Z*. A&B Distributors; and Internet/DVD recordings.

Some, Dr. Malidoma. 1999. *The Healing Wisdom of Africa*. Penguin/Putnam, Inc., New York.

Williams, Dr. Chancellor. 1987. *The Destruction of the Black Civilization*. Third World Press, Chicago.

CPSIA information can be obtained at www.ICGtesting.com
Printed in the USA
BVOW031336021111

275103BV00001B/70/P